WOLF SECRETS

Learn to Negotiate Like a

Wall Street Tycoon

The Ligon Brothers

Michael & David Ligon

WOLF SECRETS

Copyright ©2021

The Ligon Brothers

Michael& DavidLigon

@LigonBrothers

CONTENT

Preface

Dear Entrepreneur,

Welcome to Wolf Secrets. It's Our Hope that by completely reviewing this material you will have a full understanding of what it takes to maneuver an argument or a negotiation in favor of yourself and come out Victorious. If you put these techniques into practice and use them, even in your day-to-day life, you'll be surprised at how you will be able to determine the outcome in any situation you may face.

These tactics and ideas are the result of tens of thousands of phone calls, negotiations, and trial and error. You can rest assured that we have been there and done that. There's no need for you to go through the same hard fought battles in order to find out what works best. We have done it all for you.

Wolf Secrets is designed to bring all the elements together that are needed to become a strong negotiator as well as the specific strategies and techniques necessary to maximize every negotiation, phone call, and generated lead at the highest possible level.

Hopefully you already have an understanding about how vitally important it is to be a good salesperson. If, however, you are new to this, let me take a moment to explain what I mean.

If you've never given thought to the fact that being a good salesperson and having great negotiation skills is vital to your overall success in life, then the time is now to train yourself to think that way. It is extremely important for you to realize that having a strong and confident sales skill set will be the ultimate determining factor in your eventual success or failure.

The ability to dominate the deal-making process and negotiations of that deal are vital to protecting profits at every level throughout your career.

Applying the skills and tactics you will learn here to Real Estate Investing or any other industry will surely set your place as the Alpha Wolf.

It is also important to note that we insist in using all this material with the highest ethical standards and not in a way that would persuade people to do things that would not be in their best interest.

These techniques are so powerful that you must be mindful to use them to impart good at all times.

It's our belief that having powerful sales and persuasion skills are key to creating massive wealth and success for yourself, but by using these skills, you are also able to influence others that you care about and encourage them in a powerful way to do the same.

The true Secret to negotiating is; understanding that the whole sales process is the negotiation.

If you have an ironclad process and presentation, in most cases, you will not even have to negotiate the price. And if you do have to negotiate the price, it will be very little. Understanding this will set you apart from the rest.

Negotiating is not just saved for the money aspect of a deal. When you position yourself as a person of authority and can persuade the other party to see your position as very logical, they will have no choice but to **give you money**.

Introduction

In order to be successful at Wolf Secrets, you must be committed to some basic entrepreneurial guidelines.

- The drive and determination to constantly Learn and Grow

- The ability to recognize and quickly take advantage of opportunities that are presented to you

- A burning desire to create wealth and be wealthy

- A commitment to outstanding work ethic and the ability to deliver results

I recommend that you go through this material several times and purposely put yourself in an environment where you will need to start applying this material several times a week in order for it to fully take root in your mind and subconscious.

Secret 1: A.B.R.

The old way of closing sales and persuading was thought of as the ABC method or Always Be Closing. In reality, it really should look like the ABR method;**A**lways **B**uilding **R**elationships.

Once you start to realize this, closing and confirming the closing process really only becomes about 10% of the equation. You need to be identifying the needs and presenting solutions to those that you have a relationship with.

This doesn't mean that you're going to become friends with every prospect that you meet. What it does mean is that you need to have a friendly relationship with them because friends trust each other.

Ultimately you will need their trust if you want to win that sale.

The best way of getting someone's Trust is by giving them valuable information that is useful, solution-based and giving it to them for free.

Mindset is Key!

Secret 2: Stay on Point

You must know the beginning and the end when speaking to a prospect.

What I mean is that in order to make the sale you must be talking on the topic of the sale.

So, if you're trying to sell someone a house and they start talking about their dog, you will not be able to make the sale unless you bring the topic back to the house.

The art comes in when you're trying to do this persuasively but with a conversational rhythm. You don't want the prospect to think that you don't care about what they're talking about, however, you need to stay on point as a professional in your field and the expert they need to believe you are.

Keep the conversation relevant.

For example, let's say you're trying to negotiate the sale of a house. You're discussing the terms with the potential buyer and they begin speaking about their pets.

Remember, if you're doing your job right they should feel very comfortable speaking to you, so it's understandable that they could speak about personal events in a friendly manner.

Your job is to swing the conversation back to where you want it.

So, if they are discussing the fact that they just adopted a Labrador, you would respond with something like "this is a perfect house for pets," or "that's great, have a look at this yard," or"your dog is going to love it."

This way you remain personable, yet you control the topic of the conversation and keep it on the sale of the home.

Stay on Target

Secret 3: Expertise = Rapport

You must build rapport and gather intelligence effectively.

Contrary to popular belief, you do not want to start talking about yourself or asking 100 personal questions of your prospect thinking that it will help you build rapport.

The most effective way is for your prospect to believe and see that you are an expert and you want to get them to their goal quickly and professionally.

In order to effectively gather intelligence you need to talk less and to listen to more. You have to be able to identify the key questions to ask that will be specific to the type of property or item that you're selling at that time and then let the prospect talk.

Silence is better than unnecessary conversation.

The questions you will ask need to be purposeful and will help you understand if what you were selling is a proper fit for your prospect.

If you find out through your questions that it's not a good fit, you need to end the encounter and find a different product or property for that Prospect.

If you identify that a property is not right for the prospect, let them know. Explain that it's not a good deal for them, and you'll build rapport immediately.

This is almost ensuring future sales with that buyer.

Build Rapport

Secret 4: Sell Yourself First

You must be totally convinced and confident if you want to persuade someone. In order to be confident and convinced you need absolute knowledge about what you are presenting to the prospect.

You need to be able to make the most valid and factual argument that you can about your property or product.

If you're trying to sell a buyer a house, you need to have all the details.You need to know if there are any issues with the house and other pertinent information to support your position.

Remember that the first person you need to sell is going to be yourself. If you can't sell yourself, how can you expect to sell someone else?

To ensure that you're extremely confident, you need to be knowledgeable. Take the time to research, study and learn about what it is you're selling.

You don't have to get a degree in the product, just have enough knowledge to be able to articulate your opinion properly.

You want to insure that you know enough where you don't get tripped up if you're asked a question. You may also need to hammer home some key points about what it is you're selling. Therefore, do the research, know the product or service.

You don't have to "be" an expert as long as they "think" you're an expert.

Always remember, almost everything in life revolves around sales. You're either selling yourself, a product or a service, or you're being sold a product, service or trust in a person.

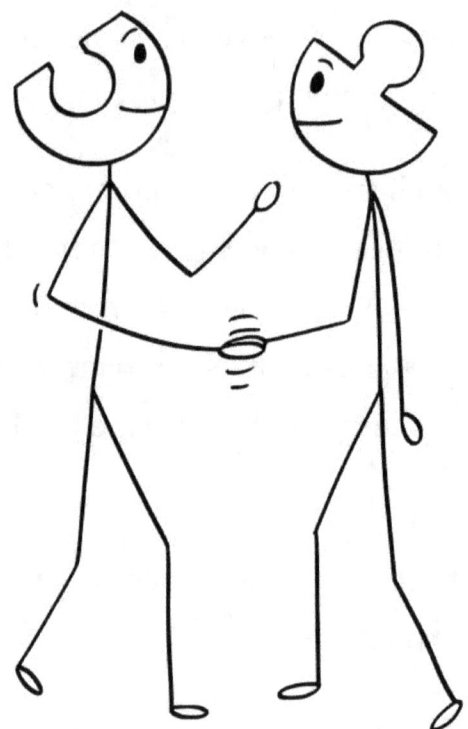

Have the Answers

Secret 5: To Sell or To Be Sold

(That is the Question)

There are two types of people: those that sell and those that get sold. Which one are you? Remember, you will be in a sell or be sold situation of some sort every day of your life.

Recognizing this and having the ability to recognize these situations, even the subtle ones, will put you far ahead of the opponent. The opponent is of course "being sold."

Think of a common and typical conversation that many of us have with our significant others in our lives. "What do you want to eat for dinner?" Even in this innocent scenario someone will be sold on what's for dinner....

In the end, this won't have a major impact but it is an illustration of the importance of recognizing these situations.

When you apply the sell or be sold concept to even these basic day-to-day scenarios you can start to realize how vitally important they are to apply them during the sales process.

Keep in mind as you're talking with prospects that in every part of the conversation there will be opportunities for you to sell the other party on why you should continue moving to the close.

Stay sharp and don't let yourself be sold on why a property is not good for your prospect unless you are the one that makes that determination.

Sell or be Sold

Secret 6: Understand Your Prospect

Having the right Prospect is vital to the sales process. You must be able to identify this key point if you want to save your valuable time for the right Prospect. You will run into three major types of buyers. They are as follows:

Ready to buy Now:

One or two out of about 10 perspective buyers will be in this category. This means that they are capable, they are ready, and they are just looking for the right situation. In this column, even those with limited persuasive and sales experience can put this buyer over the edge and make the sale.

Still Shopping but Almost Ready to Buy:

Two or three out of about 10 of your potential buyers will fall under this category. These buyers are almost ready. They're probably in a situation where they're about to free up some money in order to make a purchase.

Maybe they have a property for sale and it should be closing soon and they know they will need to buy again shortly in order to keep their business going. These buyers require a frequent touch and since they have extra time they will be looking for a better deal.

Interested but still learning and Curious:

Five or six out of about 10 buyers will be in this category. Even though they are not active buyers right now, these will be vital to building your future business.

They will become buyers if you build a relationship with them. You should make it a point to follow up with them regularly and offer them valuable and free information about what they are pursuing.

Give Info & They Will Eventually Buy

Secret 7: Scales of Justice

When you think of closing a sale, think of it as if you were to visualize the scales of Justice.

One side is the negative possible outcomes that the buyer is holding onto as reasons not to buy.

The other side is the positive reasons that they have come up with or that you have implanted in them as to why they should buy.

Your job, should you choose to accept it, is to tip the scales by removing the negative and enforcing the positive whenever possible.

Every time that you're able to remove a negative thought or belief that the buyer is holding onto off of the negative side of the scale and over to the positive side of the scale means that you are moving closer to the close.

This is why it's so important to keep the conversation relevant do the sale at hand so you can gather valuable intelligence about the current position of the scale.

Learn how to control the conversation, yet keep it flowing. Being a Master Negotiator is a true art form.

You don't have to be born with a silver tongue.You can learn this art but it will take practice. If you look hard enough you'll see opportunities in your everyday life to practice tipping the scale. It's not always about the big sale. Sometimes it's about a spot in line at your local department store, or a discount on an item at a flea market or even asking your boss for a raise.

You can use these tactics and strategies everywhere.

Secret 8: 3- to -5 Rule

When you know you are moving into a sales process with a prospect, you must make your best and strongest case within the first 5 Seconds. The way I accomplish this is by using the 3 - to - 5 rule.

You must mention three positive things, outcomes, results etc., that the buyer would get when they say yes.

The key to this is applying from the things we've already gone over, one of which is being confident and an expert. You need to already know the key factors that you would be able to include as positive things prior to making that call or having that meeting.

From that point in the conversation on, you're going back to tipping the scale and keeping the prospect on topic.

These three things could be as simple as the prospect seeing that you are as sharp as a tack, an expert, that you have authority, confidence and knowledge, and that you are excessively enthusiastic about what it is you do.

In fact, those are three components that you need to master and carry through every conversation and sales encounter you ever have.

For example, if you've done your research you will already know what the typical objections are for whatever you are selling. So, in the first 3 to 5 seconds, hit them all with a positive spin.

Let's say you're selling a house and through your research you know that the typical objections are; *it's small, close to a noisy highway and there's no pool.*

Your very first set of comments should be, *this is a great cozy little home, excellent access to major roads to get you all over town and just minutes from a community center with a pool and spa...*

Secret 9: Attention Class

I think of the old saying "the squeaky wheel gets the grease." If you allow the prospect to become the squeaky wheel, you have no choice but to become the grease yourself and give him what he wants, which is for you to accept a no.

This doesn't mean that you need to be louder or speak more. In fact, this often means that you need to speak less and allow the prospect to vent if that's what's needed.

Just remember that in order for you to get the sale you must have their attention and this isn't done my being loud or obnoxious.

This is done by being captivating, knowledgeable, and being an expert that's as sharp as a tack.

If your prospect is one of these squeaky wheels, let them talk. This will give you time to gather valuable intelligence into their negative beliefs and opinions.

You can then begin to knock down each one of those objections. The goal is to put a positive spin on any objection they may have. If you do this properly, that will leave them with only one outcome. The one you created.

At that point you can finish tipping the scales in your direction and close the deal.

Secret 10: Learn to Listen

You must go into every call with the intention of listening more than speaking. Make sure to show empathy and understanding when your prospect is talking to you. Here are a couple of things you can say that will enforce this concept.

- o Tell me everything.

- o Thanks for sharing that.

- o What else?

- o I got it.

- o Please tell me.

- o Let me write this down.

You have to acknowledge when your prospect or buyer believe they are making a valid point. Again I want to make sure I reinforce the concept of Ethics here. These tactics are very powerful and you can easily persuade someone to do something that may not be in their best interest.

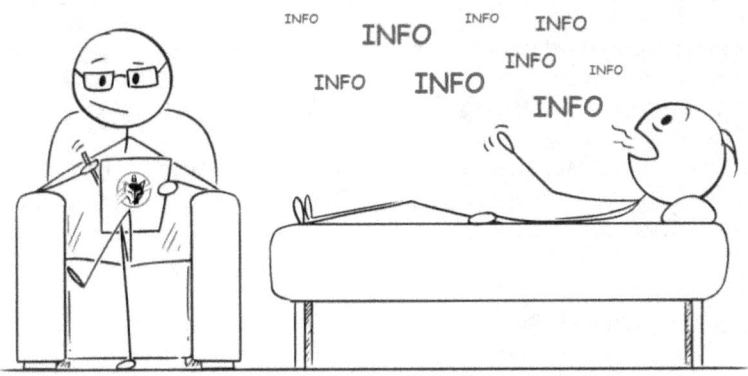

This is not what this is used for. If you find out at any point in the sales process that your product or that this property would be a bad fit for the buyer, you need to end the encounter and find them a property that would fit them.

Understanding this we'll build instant rapport and guarantee you future business.

Secret 11: Defeating Objections

In order to be a master at negotiating throughout the entire sales process, you need to have a keen understanding on how to defeat objections. You need to make sure that you hear and understand clearly what their objection is.

Step one is to listen to what they tell you. Let's say they tell you they don't have enough cash to pay for the property right now.

Step two is to acknowledge their objection. You would say something like "I understand" and "I can try to get you access to the cash you might need for this purchase."

Step three would be isolating this objection to make sure that it's really the only problem. You would say something like, "to make sure we're on the same page, is not having all the cash the

only thing that would stop you from putting the
deal together?"

Defeat Objections

From here you're going to listen and find out if that is the only thing stopping them from putting the deal together.

If not, you'll repeat this process for anything else they tell you that may be an objection until you determine what the true reason that they're telling you no is.

If you continue to cycle them through the conversation knocking down their objections, you'll eventually find the core issue, or they'll talk themselves right out of objections.

Either way, at that point, you'll start the close and get the deal done.

Secret 12: Hear Me Complain

You need to understand that often times when a buyer is talking to you and giving you what may seem like objections they are actually just complaints.

When you become proficient at identifying when an objection is actually just a complaint, you will start to master negotiating. This will allow you to close many more deals than you could possibly imagine.

However, it is a skill that takes some time to master. If you use this tactic on an actual complaint, it will be construed as insensitive or maybe even arrogant.

Having said that, if you determine that an objection is actually just a complaint, you would just acknowledge and agree with the complaint and continue right on with your close.

Complaints or Objections?

As an example, let's say a buyer says that they really don't like the street that a property is on because some of the houses are ugly...

To me this is just a complaint and not a true objection that would stop someone from buying this house.

I would simply agree and tell them "Yeah. I know. It's amazing how some people don't have pride of ownership".At this point, depending on where you are in the sales process, you would either go for the close and ask them for their signature or name for the agreement or you would continue your sales process to the next step.

Secret 13: Enthusiasm

This is where you start to understand the importance of the tone of your voice at different parts of your sales process.

When you're first telling somebody about a house or opportunity, you need to sound excited. Be very concise, confident and enthusiastic.

You have to remember that people want to relate to other people and they do it subconsciously whether they like it or not.

So when you're talking while being enthusiastic, confident and excited, your prospect will naturally pick up on these emotions and follow along.

This will add to the momentum of your sales process and bring them further along down the closing line, which will allow you to build and build on this momentum.

The best way to accomplish this is to start by matching the prospects enthusiasm and tone, then elevating it slowly to bring it to where you want to be.

When you do this correctly, it's a completely unnoticeable change in the conversation, yet the prospect will be more enthusiastic and also view you as more trustworthy than before.

The change in enthusiasm invokes a primal connection of trust.

Build Trust

Secret 14: Speak With C.A.R.E.

(Cadence, Accentuation, Rhythm, Emphasis)

If you want to make any presentation very powerful and convincing you need to learn the key points of when you should drop your tone and almost whisper.

Naturally, when people hear a whisper, they tune in very intently to hear what you're saying, as if you're telling them a secret.

This invokes a natural state of curiosity in the prospect. Think about it.Who doesn't want to know and be let in on a secret?

You want to use this concept when introducing the price or a discounted price or maybe some great feature about the property that they didn't know about. Maybe you were going to tell them how the area is "super hot" right now.

Speak with C.A.R.E.

Picture this so you can have a visual representation of what this would look like even if you're talking with someone on the phone.

You have a client in front of you on the other side of your desk.You want to make a dramatic point to them so you would lean forward, look side to side to make sure no one else is listening, and almost whisper this Revelation to them.

This is very powerful in person but you still can use this tactic on the phone because people would hear it in the tone of your voice and be intently listening to what comes out of your mouth next.

Secret 15: Have a Script

Do not overlook the importance of having a script. All great generals have a battle plan when they're going into war.

And remember what I said previously; every part of your sales process is a negotiation. The stronger you are in the beginning, the less actual negotiations will need to be done on the price.

You need to realize that price is very seldom the main objection but is very often used as a scapegoat and complained about.

It's vitally important to have a script because your prospect will constantly be taking you away from it and you need to have something to return to.

Secret 16: Know the "3"s

One:

Thebuyer must love and trust you. Now this comes easy if you have a long relationship with somebody. But how do you accomplish this with a New Prospect? They have to believe that you have their best interest in mind even if this might mean that you tell them that this isn't the right deal for them. They have to know that you're being truthful and honest; always practice honesty and ethics in your conversation and trust should come naturally.

Always disclose information about the property that you know even if it's not great for the sale because they may know about it already. This will solidify you as an honest person in their mind, which you should be.

Two:

They must love the property. This is where your script comes into play.You can make sure you're identifying the key points as you talk with them and if this deal is right for them it should be obvious and you should be able to move straight into the close.

Three:

They must love and trust your company. If you're just starting out there are certain things you can do to overcome this "must." You can be associated with another company that they know.

Also, letting them know that they are more than welcome to have their attorney review any paperwork that would be used and that their attorney could also work with your processors to ensure that everything is as you say it is, should get the deal closed.

This will go a long way in building Goodwill and ultimately will build that love and Trust in your brand and Company.

You'll also want to tell them that your company is newer and that your purpose is to build long-term relationships. You want to make sure that this property is a good fit to them and if not, you don't want to try and force it.Be happy to move on and find something better.

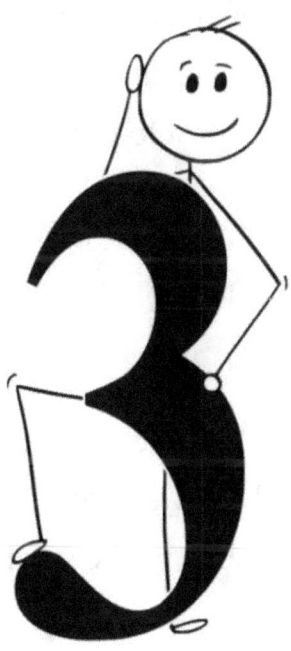

Secret 17: Mirror/Match

Be subtle when using this tactic as you don't want to be seen as disingenuous. When done correctly, this is another tool that will be used to build rapport.A strong Rapport means a stronger negotiating position.

Simply stated, this is using similar body language and speech patterns as your prospect. Picture this as an extreme example to illustrate what I mean by mirroring and matching. If you're sitting in front of an elderly Prospect who is speaking to you slowly and is sitting very relaxed in their chair almost lounging...

You would not want to be fidgety, bouncing around in your chair and talking very quickly to them.

This would likely make them very uncomfortable. You don't want to be seen as a Slick Banker. You want to be seen as the grandchild. Now this doesn't mean that you will abandon your scripts, stay on point.

You just want to make sure that you use the appropriate Wolf tactics on the appropriate people. All these tactics work, however, some work better on some people than others. Identify your prospect and use the correct tactics to close the deal.

Secret 18: FutureCast

As you're gathering intelligence, building rapport with the proper questions while being confident and professional, you will want to use what we call FutureCasting. You need to be helping your buyer to realize the benefits they will have from closing this deal with you. It is important to have proper timing when using this tactic

You do not want to FutureCast too early. At least, not before you had the chance to gather intelligence and motive from your buyer.

In real estate, if the buyer is an investor and plans to fix and flip the property, this may look something like this:

Tell them how quickly properties sell in this area once they're rehabbed or that there's very low inventory because it's a hot area.

This will begin the process in their mind of envisioning quickly receiving their profits from this deal. The key point is to always look for opportunities to FutureCast.

Whenever you can give a prospect a thought of a positive outcome, it will always work in your favor.

Secret 19: The Redirect

When trying to keep a buyer on point and on task and focused on the sale, it will be necessary at points to redirect. Make sure that when doing this, you're using the tactics you've been shown with tone and body language.

You don't want to seem like you are being pushy or uncaring. Always do this with the utmost respect and sincerity. You do not want to interrupt or try to quiet down the buyer.

Let's say that a prospect starts randomly talking to you about a fishing trip he took over the weekend or this past weekend's football game, etc.

You want to acknowledge, briefly engage in a relative manner and then redirect back to the script.

This could be saying something like: I heard that was a great game, who won again?

Oh that's great, well I can picture a great room here for watching games once the house is rehabbed. Let me ask you a question, do you do a lot of deals in this area?

Keep in mind that being an expert, a professional, and as sharp as a tack is what your buyer wants from you and that will be accomplished by acknowledging, engaging then redirecting

Chapter 20: Listen / Talk Less

He will often be tempted after asking the buyer a question to fill the void of silence as they try to answer you. Never do this. If you ask a question, before you speak again, you need to get a response.

If you're a talkative or nervous person, this may be very difficult in the beginning. It is however very important that you practice this in every conversation.

Never give the buyer options and answers to question you just asked.

SPEAK LESS   LISTEN MORE

All this is doing is giving them an easy way out, and in turn you are subverting your own investigation.

Never ever answer for the buyer. When you are in the fact-finding phase, you should be intently listening and speaking less than the buyer is.

When you become good at asking the right questions, often times the buyers will even paint themselves into a corner, and they may realize that they really have no reason not to just close the sale.

Remember, most people don't like silence in a conversation. Even a person that's not normally a talkative person will open up if you set the tone correctly. Give short relaxed answers and always end with a question to keep the conversation going until you've gathered enough intel.

Identifying Personalities

Ok, so now you know the secrets that the Pros use to master a negotiation.

Now, it's time to develop the tools you need to become a Master Negotiator. First things first; identify the individual's personality.

Every person has a distinct personality type and buying decision behavior. As a Master Negotiator, you need to be able to identify these personalities. Here are the 4 distinct prominent personality types:

1) – The Analytical (*The Thinker*)
2) – The Expressive (*The Knower*)
3) – The Driver (*The Alpha*)
4) – The Amiable (*The Feeler*)

There will be an instance where you'll meet someone that border lines two or more personality types, but there is always one dominant trait.

Identify the Personality

The Thinker

The Thinker is someone who is analytical and looks for facts and data to make a decision.

When negotiating with a Thinker you need to be on your "A" game. You should always do your research and know what you are selling, but with an Analytical person, you'll need to be able to come across as "all knowing".

This personality type will argue about quality, efficiency and facts about the functionality, benefits or lack thereof of a product or service.

You need to be able to supply them with a deeper understanding and knowledge of what you are offering. Thinkers put logic before emotion, so your typical emotional close won't work on analytical personality types.

Be prepared to answer questions and don't be afraid to supply them with an abundance of data and information. The more detail you can provide, the more of an expert you will appear to be. When negotiating with this personality type you need to be viewed as "The Expert".

Be ready for a long negotiation. Analytical thinkers take their time making decisions.

The Thinker

Tell me more!

Workbook Option

It's time to train your brain to identify Personality types.

Think about someone you know or have met that fits the description of a Thinker Personality type and enter the details:

Name:_____

What traits do they exhibit to classify them as a Thinker Personality Type?

_____

_____

_____

_____

_____

_____

_____

_____

_____

_____

_____

This person should be extremely analytical and data driven. They make decisions based on facts and figures.

The Knower

The Knower is someone who thinks they know best. They love to voice their own opinion on everything.

When negotiating with a Knower, you don't want to bombard them with facts and information like you would a Thinker. They already believe that they know best. The best way to negotiate with this personality type is to create a story. You want to create a picture in their mind of their desired outcome.

A story with well-placed metaphors will allow them to believe that what you are offering will provide them with the outcome they seek. The key is to tell a story relevant to their desired outcome. This way you will invoke an emotional connection. The Knower will make a decision based more on emotion than on logic.

The Knower

I know Best!

Since emotion is the driving factor for this personality type, they normally decide quickly. So in many instances, you can close a knower in your first encounter.

One important thing to remember is that the Knower doesn't like to feel as if you are teaching them.

You need to be knowledgeable and an expert in every negotiation, but a Knower has done research and thinks they know what they need to know.

You job in this negotiation is to navigate them using their positive views on the subject, diverting their attention away from their negative views all while reassuring them that they will get the outcome they desire.

When this is done properly you can close 100% of all Knowers on the spot.

Workbook Option

It's time to train your brain to identify Personality types.

Think about someone you know or have met that fits the description of a Knower Personality type and enter the details:

Name:_____

What traits do they exhibit to classify them as a Knower Personality Type?

_____

_____

_____

_____

_____

_____

_____

_____

_____

_____

_____

This person should be a bit of a know-it-all and extremely opinionated. They make decisions based more on emotion that logic

The Alpha

The Alpha is someone who is self-centered and confident. These personality types are sometimes aggressive and combative.

By nature, an Alpha personality is commanding and motivated to achieve their desired outcome.

When negotiating with an Alpha personality, you must stand your ground. Be assertive yet accepting of their opinions and perspective on the topic.

An Alpha wants to believe that they are in control of the negotiation. Let them.

Unlike Thinkers who need a long negotiation, or Knowers who will entertain a story or long drawn out details, an Alpha wants you to get to the point.

Don't waste time trying to explain your position. Get straight to the offer and get ready for the objections.

Negotiations with an Alpha can be very easy and also very hard. They are quick to make a decision but they need to feel as if they were the ones that ultimately made the decision.

If they feel as if they are being convinced, you will surly get extreme push back and the deal can fall apart.

You can expect an Alpha to try and trip you up and manipulate the negotiation. They want to appear sharp and just as capable as you if not more capable.

Your best bet when negotiation with an Alpha is to provide solid information about why they should say yes; and then hammer home what your service or offer can do for them and how much better they will make out because they went with you.

Use metaphors and analogies to get your points across. This way, you're not telling them what you offer. You're allowing them to deduce the outcome based on quick references.

Alphas are quick thinkers. Give them carefully worded nuggets of information and let them come to the conclusion that they must have whatever you are offering.

Be prepared for a battle. Most Alphas like a little confrontation and tend to enjoy a little verbal wrestling.

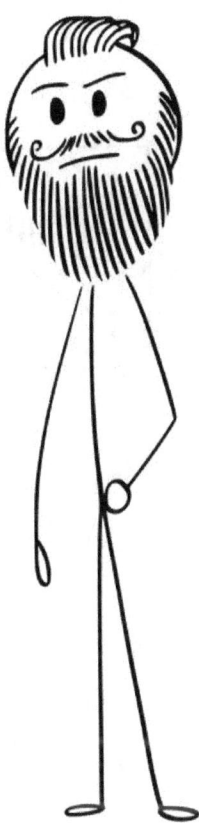

The Alpha

I'm the Boss!

Workbook Option

Train Your Brain

It's time to train your brain to identify Personality types.

Think about someone you know or have met that fits the description of an Alpha Personality type and enter the details:

Name:_____

What traits do they exhibit to clasify them as an Alpha Personality Type?

_____

_____

_____

_____

_____

_____

_____

_____

_____

_____

_____

This person should be confident and secure in their opinions. They make decisions based on their belief that the product or service will allow them to reach their desired outcome.

The Feeler

The Feeler is someone who needs to like you. They need to feel that you are trustworthy.

When negotiating with a Feeler, you'll need to make a good impression. The Feeler will make the majority of their decisions purely on emotion.

They are not logical thinkers. That's not to say they aren't intelligent. They can be extremely intelligent. The fact still remains that you will not close a Feeler personality type if they do not like you. They can be completely sold on the idea that whatever you have will solve their issue, and you will still not close the deal.

They'll take that new found knowledge and all your negotiating work and find a competitor that they do like and buy from them.

It is extremely important that you make a connection with this personality type.

You want to ask a Feeler questions that allows them to tell you a story. Get them talking about their experiences and how your offer may positively affect them on a personal level.

If your offer is more business based, getthem to open up about their expectations and desired outcomes with your offer. FurtureCasting this type of personality is a great way to build rapport.

Remember, the number one goal with a Feeler is to make sure they like and trust you. To make a person like you, you need to make them feel valued. So address their needs and desires.

Be compassionate. Feeler personality types normally want to think of the transaction as building on a long term relationship with you or your firm.

Be prepared for a long negotiation and deep conversations with this personality type.

Unlike an Alpha personality type where you need to get to the point and fast, with a Feeler, you can allow the conversation to stray off topic just a little bit as you collect valuable data.

This will give you ammo that will assist in building a deeper connection. Just make sure you don't lose site of the overall goal of closing the sale.

During every interaction and every conversation you have with any potential customer, you must always be ready to throw in a close!

The Feeler

Let's be friends.

Workbook Option

It's time to train your brain to identify Personality types.

Think about someone you know or have met that fits the description of a Feeler Personality type and enter the details:

Name:_____

What traits do they exhibit to classify them as a Feeler Personality Type?

_____

_____

_____

_____

_____

_____

_____

_____

_____

_____

_____

This person should be emotional and kind. They believe themselves to be trustworthy and expect the same from others. They make decisions based primarily on emotion rather than logic.

Power Closes

The Close is the most important part of any negotiation. There are numerous ways to close a sale, but it all boils down to 3 primary closes.

1) – The Soft Close (or) Trial Close

2) – The Direct Close

3) – The Hammer Close

All of these closes use four basic fundamentals.

1) – Particular words and phrases that help influence and motivate the close

2) - Different tones and cadences that emphasize your enthusiasm to close

3) – Infinity patterns that keep you on track to close

4) – Defusers that allow you to target and eliminate objections.

Power Closes

Let's make a Deal!

Trial Closes

The "Soft close," also known as "Trial close," can be used at any time during a negotiation. It's a very subtle way to steer the negotiation in your direction by invoking positive feedback.

Here's an example of a negotiation and the use of a trial close;

Prospect: *I'm not sure if this is the product/service that is right for me.*

Wolf Negotiator (You): *If you give me a few minutes of your time, I can tell you exactly how this service/product will (enter benefit) you. How's that sound?*

In this particular example, the trial close is "*How's that sound*". It's a simple phrase that causes the prospect to say something positive like "ok sure" or "sounds good"

These little trial closes are extremely important during the negotiation. Everyone wants to say no. That's everyone's first reaction, so you have to get passed the first few no's and get to the real objections.

As you're being told no, if you drop these trial closes, you'll keep the negotiation on a positive note. Here's another example:

Prospect: *"It's too expensive or I can't afford it."*

Wolf Negotiator (You): *"I'd hate for you to lose out so how about we work around what you can afford. Fair enough?"*

In this particular example, the trial close is *"Fair enough?"*. If you get in the habit of dropping these phrases, you'll be surprised at how easy it is to elevate the prospect's enthusiasm during the conversation.

You'll start by hear things like,"sure" and "yeah ,why not" then it will turn into "wow, thanks" and "that's awesome."

Remember that the word No is inevitable. Get to your first no as soon as you can.Drop a few trial closes to change the tone of the negotiation and then, when the time is right, go for the Close!

Trail Closes
Sound good...

The Direct Close

The "Direct close" is a little different than just throwing in a few phrases to build enthusiasm and rapport with your prospect.

You'll use this close when you've negotiated to a point where you're ready to get the sale. You've already received a few "nos" and you've dealt with a few objections and now it's time to close the sale.

Here's an example of a "Direct close":

Prospect: *"It all sounds good, but I need to think about it."*

Wolf Negotiator (You): *"We can both agree that successful people are action takers, right? (wait for inevitable yes) You said it yourself.It sounds great and that's because it is. Let's get it done and get you on your way to (enter benefit here). We have two payment options, which one works for you?*

With a direct close, you'll end up directly asking for the sale after your rebuttal to the last objection.

It's important to hold the direct close until after you've used a few of the Wolf Secrets as well as several trial closes. This will insure that you don't come across as pushy.

The use of these Secrets and the act of dropping trial closes throughout the negotiation will create an enthusiastic and positive environment. By this point, they've agreed with you several times and it makes it harder to say no when you introduce the direct close.

Don't be afraid to ask for payment (if selling a product) or whatever it is that you are negotiating about at this point. Hit them with a Direct Close and then wait. Do not speak first, wait for them to respond to your Close.

If after all the Secrets and Trial Closes you still get a No on your Direct Close, it's time for The Hammer Close.

Remember that the negotiation is never over. As long as your prospect is still listening, whether it is on the phone or in person, it's not over.

This is where you'll continue your infinity patterns, which we'll explain in the next chapter. Every good negotiation will consist of a healthy back and forth of objections and rebuttals.

You job is not to wear down your prospect; you want to genuinely show them why your product or service is right for them.

Direct Closes

Let's do this!

The Hammer Close

The "Hammer close" is a forceful close. If you've tried it all; trial closes, secrets, direct closes and you're still not able to close the deal, but the prospect is still engaging with you, then it's time to drop the Hammer!

Here's an example of a "Hammer Close":

Prospect: *"Another Objection (any objection)"*

Wolf Negotiator (You): *"Look, you don't know me and probably don't trust me. That's ok. I would feel the same way. But the fact is that this is great for you and you know it. If I was an old friend and I was recommending this (product/service) you would have pulled the trigger already. Don't let doubt stop you from (benefit). Pull the trigger and let's get you started. Sound good?*

Two things are happening in this example provided. One: you are acknowledging and exposing the fact that your prospect doesn't trust you. You're making that objection well known. It's no longer a subconscious thought.

This is important! The number one reason a closer can't make a conversion is because of Trust. If deep down they don't trust you, you won't make a sale.

Two: you're demanding a decision. *"Pull the trigger and let's get you started."* The pull the trigger portion of the close is a direct call to action. If you've been negotiating for a while and you're getting nowhere, you need to be able to drop a few hammers and try and push the close.

Don't be afraid to drop a Hammer at anytime in the conversation where you feel a direct call to action may close it. They can even come across as subtle as, "*Oh man! You need to get this right now. Do you have your credit card on you?"* A good time to drop a Hammer close is when the prospect has told you something positive about what you are offering, like a positive remark or story on how it would benefit them.

A Hammer Close doesn't always have to be the last resort, but it's forceful so use it wisely.

Here's an example of a hammer close dropped in during the early parts of a negotiation:

Prospect: *"This would be great for my business; I could (enter benefit)"*

Wolf Negotiator (You): *"You need to do this now. Why are we even still talking about it (laughingly).What do you prefer Visa or MasterCard?*

Hammer closes are also great to use with metaphors. All good Negotiators know that metaphors are an excellent way to build rapport with a prospect.

Metaphors paint a picture and allow the prospect to see him benefiting from the product or service through a story that they can identify with.

Using a Hammer close in combination with a metaphor, story or during positive feedback can sometimes fast track your close.

In some instances, the enthusiasm can be so high that when a Hammer close is dropped, the prospect can't say no. At a high point of a conversation, a simple *"Ok, that's it, we're doing this right now"* can be an excellent Hammer Close to get the deal done.

The Hammer close is definitely a more forceful close and normally includes a hard call to action, but when done right and at the appropriate time, it works great!

Hammer Closes

What are you waiting for?

Infinity Patterns

Infinity Patterns are an essential part of any successful negotiation. You need to be able to navigate every conversation and control the outcome.

With Infinity Patterns, you can allow the prospect to slide off topic in an effort to build a personal rapport, and then bring them back on track.

You can also use Infinity Patterns to consistently push closes on your prospect throughout the entire negotiation.

Here's an example of an "Infinity Pattern":

Prospect: *(off topic story or comment)* *"Sorry for the noise, my washer is broken so it's really loud"*

Wolf Negotiator (You): *"No worries, funny story, I tried to fix my own washer once and forgot to turn off the water, ended up flooding my whole apartment (laughingly).That taught me why it's so important to have the right knowledge for the job, and that's what we offer when it comes to (product/service).Drop trial close.*

Prospect: *(still off topic) "I need to get it fixed before I have the same issue."*

Wolf Negotiator (You): *"It helps to have extra cash and some residual income coming in for these types of issues. I can't tell you how many of our clients benefit from (product/service).Let's get you started and you can have that issue resolved in no time. Sound Good?"* (Trial close)

In this example, the infinity pattern is used to circle back around to the main objective, which is to close the client. You can see that with each rapport building story or metaphor, the Negotiator brings the conversation back to the benefit or the product or service being offered.

Infinity patterns are used continuously through ever single negotiation. You can also isolate infinity patterns and use them with only Closes.

Essentially what this means is that every time you eliminate an objection, you reintegrate the benefit of your product or service and insert a Close immediately.

The goal in every negotiation is to close as quickly as possible, but in order to close you must build Trust. Building trust takes time and you'll need to go off topic sometimes in order to find similarities and common ground in which to build off of.

The use of metaphors and stories is an excellent way to bond with your prospect, but they will normally change the course of the conversation from a negotiation to a friendly dialog.

This is why infinity patterns are so important. They allow you to go off topic and immediately return to the goal of closing the prospect.

Remember that there are several different roads you can take to get to your destination, but you have to remain focused on the end goal: closing the Prospect!

Make sure you use Infinity Patters in all your negotiations.Become an expert at building trust and rapport all while bringing your prospect back to the close whenever youfeel it's time.

This is a talent that when mastered can be mesmerizing to a prospect.

Infinity Patterns

Circle Back & Close

Overcoming Objections

Objections are normally just complaints that haven't been addressed yet. It's inevitable. You will hear several "Nos" when negotiating with prospects.

The goal is to get to the first no as soon as possible and then begin breaking down the prospects negative views and complaints to find their true objections.

There are four typical objections:

1) – Lack of Urgency
2) – Lack of Need
3) – Lack of Budget
4) – Lack of Trust

Let's breakdown each one of the four common objections and determine the best way to handle them.

Lack of Urgency

The Lack of Urgency objection is normally used when a person likes the product/service but doesn't have an immediate need for it.

Even if the prospect sees the benefit, they may still be hesitant to pull the trigger simply because they don't need it at that moment.

The first thing you want to do is identify if the timing is actually the issue. Sometimes one objection is just masking another one. Make sure you get the prospect to explain with a bit of detail why timing is an issue for them.

This allows you to gather Intel and make the determination of whether the timing is indeed the primary objection. If it is, timing is one of the easiest objections to overcome.

When a prospect has shown that they are of your work is already done.

The most common method to deal with the lack of urgency objection is with the *"what could have been"* rebuttal.

You'll need to paint a picture of what could have been if they had made a decision in their life before they thought they needed it.

For instance, you could tell your prospect:

"Sometimes knowing that something is great and taking advantage of it are two different things. If you could go back in time and buy Apple stock when it first came out, you'd be a quadrillionaire right now. It's better to be an action taker now, then to feel the pain of regret later. I say you jump on this today, how's that sound?"

With the statement above, you've accomplished several things. You highlighted an already existing regret and you've placed the fear of missing out in the prospect's head.

The goal is to invoke an emotional response to *what could have been* with details, stories and metaphors of things that the prospect can immediately relate with.

If you can do this correctly, the prospect will feel that they've already missed out on several great things and they won't want to miss out on this one.

Make sure you throw in some FutureCasting and elaborate on the benefits of acting now rather than later and you should be able to close the deal.

Lack of Urgency

Do I need it now?

Lack of Need

The Lack of Need objection is normally used when a person can't see the how the product/service will benefit them or their lives.

On the surface, this may seem like a dead-end, but the truth is that this objection is normally more of a complaint than an objection.

The Lack of Need objection is basically just the prospect thinking *"How will this benefit me?"* As a Master negotiator, this is a perfect time to use your bag of tactics to enlighten the prospect as to why they must have your product or service.

This is your opportunity to provide them information about your offer as well as bombard them with the infinite benefits of your product/service.

Remember that you can't convince someone to buy something that they don't need. The goal is to show them that they absolutely need what you are offering. This can be accomplished by collecting as much information as possible on the prospects "pain points."

A "pain point" is an issue that your prospect has that they need a remedy to. Show them that their remedy is you, your product or your service.

For example; let's say your prospect has a car dealership and you are offering landscaping services.

If the prospect already has a landscaping company, there is no pain point for them, and they won't see the value of your service.

However, if you've done your research on your prospect, than you may know that they have several trees on their car lot, and those trees have several bird nests on them. And because of all the birds they constantly have to pay money to their crews to have the cars washed and windows cleaned form all the bird droppings.

Well, with this knowledge, you may present your offer in a different manner. Instead of offering basic lawn maintenance services, you offer, Luxury landscaping Services with pest removal and relocation.

So now you've created an offer highlighting a "pain point" for a service that they never knew they actually needed. Now they can see the value in your service.

When you have a product or service, you need to collect Intel and do some research on whatever leads you are marketing to. You can create a need for your product/service in any industry and with any lead if you find their pain points.

Some prospects won't know they need your offer until you make them understand that they must have it, and how did they live without it. Then you can introduce your Wolf negotiation tactics and close the deal.

Never let a Lack of Need objection stop you from creating a need for your product. Remember, everyone needs what you have to offer, they just don't know it yet!

metaphors painting a clear picture of the value and benefit of the product/service you are offering.

Stories about how you or a loved one benefited from your offer. Creating "comparison values" on your product or service is an excellent way to justify the expense to a prospect.

You begin by finding familiar items that are priced higher than your offer and then you compare them to your product/service in a manner that makes it seems as if it's a no brainer to go with your offer.

The items don't even need to make sense. They just need to have higher values and be things that the prospect can relate to.

Here's an example of how to do a "comparison value" in a negotiation:

"I wish everyone saw the value in investing in themselves.Did you know that the average person spend over $4,000 dollars a year on fast food? Just imagine what they could do if they used that money to invest in their future?"

In this "comparison value," you're comparing a familiar item (fast food) with the fact that most people have the money to spend thousands each year on fast food yet come up with excuses not to invest in themselves.

Comparison values like this dropped into your negotiation help justify the expense. People can relate to expenses that they are already paying for, especially ones that they are getting no real value out of. So when you compare your offer with a familiar expense it assists in justifying the validity of your product/service.

Another way to combat the Lack of Budget objection is to make your offer seem so good that they feel they need to find the money.

Often times, when a person says *"I can't afford this,"* they don't truly mean it. It's just beyond what they feel comfortable spending for whatever it is that you are offering.

The goal is to make the prospect understand that it will ultimately cost them more money in the long run if they don't take advantage of your offer.

You need to be able to close everyone who is closable. Not everyone is closable; the Lack of Budget objection is sometimes exactly that. The prospect just doesn't have the funds to close.

A Master Negotiator will find a way to insure that the prospect can get the money elsewhere. Your job is to close deals and you should only be offering products and services that can better someone's life. Since that's the case, it's ok to dig in and see if you can find other avenues for the prospect to find the money to close the deal.

If it's a physical product, maybe you can offer financing or payment plans. If it's a service, maybe you can offer layaway or break the payment up as parts of the services are completed.

It's your job to think outside the box and get the deal closed. Just because the objection is Lack of Budget, that doesn't mean you give up. The question then becomes, what can you pay, or how can you pay or where can you get the money to pay.

Once you've been negotiating for a while and you've dropped some trial closes and cleared up all the other objections, if cost is the only objection left, don't be afraid to give the prospect ideas on how to fund your product or service.

A really good closing tactic for cost is the Credit Card Finance Close.

Tell your prospect; *"you can finance the purchase through your credit card company. Make the payment today and all you have to do is make your regular monthly payments to pay it off".*

You'd be surprised how many times this close works. It's all about how it's framed. The prospect most likely would have used a credit card to fund the transaction anyway, but when you,*the Mater Negotiator*, provide them with the idea of the credit t card company financing the deal for them, it changes their view on the transaction.

Now it's not viewed as a $$$$ lump purchase. It's viewed as an affordable Monthly charge. The Lack of Budget objection is like any other. You need show the prospect the value, while minimizing the risk and be prepared to offer payment options or find solutions for them to fund the deal.

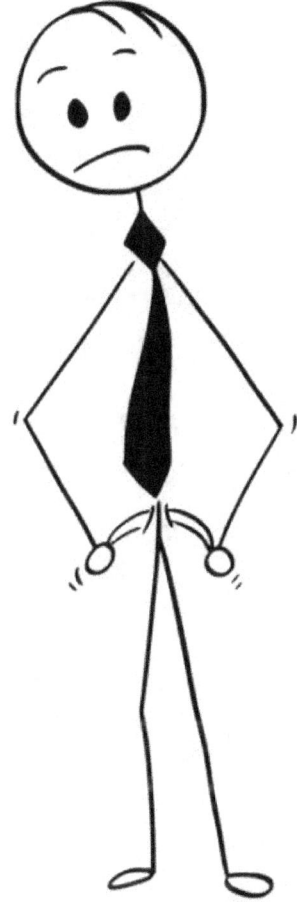

Lack of Budget

I don't have the money

Lack of Trust

The Lack of Trust objection is the most important objection to overcome. If your prospect doesn't trust you, you will not be able to convert the transaction.

Trust is the number one reason people buy goods and services. Think about it like this; when you go on Amazon to buy a product, what's the first thing you do when you see a product you want? You scroll down to the reviews.

Why do people read reviews? Consumers read reviews because they want to Trust that the product or service will work for them. If it's worked for others in the manner in which they intend to use it, then they assume it will work for them.

Trust is really all you need. It will overcome any objection. Let's stack it up against the other 3 objections and see how it does.

Lack of Urgency: If your prospect doesn't really need your product or service "right now" but a family member says *"you have to get that today,"* the chances are that they will buy it. Why? Because they trust the opinion of the family member and trust outweighs logic.

Lack of Need: Even if your prospect can't see the value in your product or service, if they trust in you, they'll still get it. Think about your friend calling you up and saying *"You have to buy this coffee cup I just got. It's Awesome!"* You don't need a coffee cup. You already have three. It won't matter though. All they need to do is tell you *"Trust me, you won't be disappointed"* and BAM, off to Amazon you go.

Lack of Budget: Even if you think you're dead-broke, if a trusted friend says *"You have to go in on this deal with me. We're going to make money. Trust me."* If it's at all possible, you'll probably respond with *"Well, I guess it's going to bepeanut butter and jelly sandwiches for the next few months, but ok. I'm in."* That's the power of Trust.

Your number one Goal as a Master Negotiator is to build Trust. Everything else will follow.

How do you build trust? You use all the Secrets and tactics that we've provided you in this book to build a special connection to every prospect you interact with.

Your prospect must trust and believe that you, your service or your product is exactly what they need. No trust = No Deal. Period.

Lack of Trust

Hi, I'm Trustworthy!

Powerful One Liners

Here are 5 of the most common one-liners we use in Real Estate to squeeze a higher offer out of a buyer.

These work best when you are fairly close to agreeing on a final price.

One:

"Is that the best you can do?"*Wait for them to reply before speaking! You'd be surprised at how many people will give you a little bit more simply because you asked.*

Two:

"If we could meet at $XXX,XXX we can lock it in today, how's that sound?"

Again always wait for them to answer.

Three:

"I would like to do this deal with you. I believe my partner has a slightly higher offer than that. What's the best you can do so that I can discuss it with him right now?"

Four:

"It looks like we're really close to getting this deal done.How about we meet in the middle and lock this in right now. How's that sound?"

Five:

"I can't make any promises, but if you could do \$XXX,XXX right now, I will go fight to make it happen. Sound fair enough?"

Sign Here

What's Next?

The information we've provided in this book should give you all the tools and tactics you need to become an expert negotiator.

If you want to learn more tactics, tricks and strategies, we're here to help.

We have compiled an A-Z course on superior negotiation tactics and techniques. If you're interested in sharpening your negotiation skills even further; simply visit our Online Training Center at

www.LigonU.com

(https://www.ligonu.com/)

BONUS: 5 Keys to Success

As a bonus, here are 5 key components that every aspiring entrepreneur should know and follow to be successful.

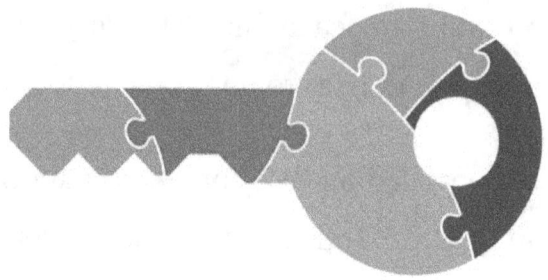

Key One:

Invest in Yourself

Successful entrepreneurs invest in their minds and their bodies. They pay for knowledge as often as possible. Acquiring knowledge allows you to accelerate your success by buying experience.

Buying experience allows you to buy time, and every successful person knows time is the only thing we can never get back.

Key Two:

Be Confident and Resourceful

Successful entrepreneurs develop confidence in their abilities. Knowledge builds confidence, and being more confident breeds healthy actions and decisions.

When you are confident in your abilities, you tend to be more resourceful with your decision making.

Key Three:

Be Self-Motivated

All successful entrepreneurs understand the importance of being self-motivated. You cannot leave your motivation up to others. Remember that not everything will always go as planned. Accept that fact, adapt and move on.

Understand that the pressure is a privilege.

Key Four:

Be Passionate

Successful entrepreneurs identify their passion points. Ask yourself: what do you feel passionate about? Is it helping others, building a network, or something else? Be passionate about your purpose. Be enthusiastic about your goals.Learn to love the journey.

This will, in turn, assist you in being self-motivated.

Key Five:

Be Willing to Risk for Profit

All successful entrepreneurs understand that you must be willing to risk in order to succeed. You must be willing to invest time and money without fullyknowing the outcome.

More often than not, there is no instant gratification. Success is a journey. You must be able to travel that journey outside your comfort zone.

Follow these 5 Keys and you will be on your way to a successful life!

Conclusion

We hope that, at the very least, we have opened your eyes to the possibility that a successful career in real estate investing is within your reach. We hope that the steps we have laid out can bring this lifestyle into reality for you and your family or your future family.

We're passionate about helping others achieve success in their life through real estate. Our LYNK Real Estate Investing System has been developed over many years and after completing, as of the time of this book, over 500 real estate transactions in one of the toughest, most competitive, brutal real estate markets in the world; Miami, Florida. Miami is notorious for being an extremely fast paced and Bellwether market in our country and the world. If you dive in and use the successful system that we have developed in this tough market, then you should be able to dominate anywhere you implement these strategies.

By dedicating yourself to achieving your dreams, using real estate as the vehicleto success and the tactics that got us to where we are today,you can gowherever your heart desires. You don't have to do it on your own. We've already made the mistakes and paved the way! Just copy what works, and success will find you right where you are. We wish you unlimited success!

"Having mentors is a must if you want to succeed. If you want to be a successful person, you have to buy knowledge and mentorships whenever possible and surround yourself with successful people!"

~ The Ligon Brothers ~

About the Authors

David Ligon   Michael Ligon

The Ligon Brothers

The Ligon Brothers are Real Estate Investors, Entrepreneurs, Coaches and Mentors.

They've taken their overwhelming experience in the field of real estate investing andnegotiations and used it to develop the Wolf Secrets Negotiation Tactics.

These techniques and tactics are used by the best of the best.

Here are some of The Ligon Brothers achievements:

2020:

Created the Millionaires Mastermind Circle

2018:

Launched the MLS Digital Flipping Method™

2017:

Developed the LYNK™ Real Estate System

2017:

Created LigonU, an online Training Center

2016:

Recipients of the "Most Deals of the Year" Award

2005:

Florida's Leading Real Estate Investment Firm

Ongoing:

Negotiated &Flipped Thousands of Real Estate Transactions

Connect with the Ligon Brothers

Facebook: @LigonBrothers

https://www.facebook.com/LigonBrothers

Instagram: @LigonBrothers

https://www.instagram.com/ligonbrothers

Linked In: @LigonBrothers

https://www.linkedin.com/company/ligonbrothers

Twitter: @LigonBrothers

https://twitter.com/ligonbrothers

Website:

https://www.ligonbrothers.com

Online Training Center:

https://www.ligonu.com/

Disclaimer

The Ligon Brothers are not CPA's, Realtors® or Attorneys. Any information that is found or derived from this documentation or any product(s), service(s), tactic(s), techniques and/or idea(s) discussed or described, is NOT to be construed as legal, medical, personal or financial advice. The information provided in the documents, videos, materials, products, websites, etc. is not to be interpreted as a guarantee and/or promise of earnings. The earning potential is solely and entirely dependent on the individual using the product(s), service(s), tactic(s), techniques and/or idea(s) discussed or described.

The Ligon Brothers cannot guarantee the success or profit potential of anyone using the product(s), service(s), tactic(s), techniques and/or idea(s) discussed or described. We cannot guarantee your success. Any and all claims made by the Ligon Brothers are to be considered as exceptional by seasoned professionals and not the average result of any person(s) that using the product(s), service(s), tactic(s), techniques and/or idea(s) discussed or described. No guarantees are made that you will achieve the same or similar results as The Ligon Brothers and/or any of their students or examples discussed.

NO GUARANTEES ARE MADE THAT ANYONE USING THE PRODUCT(S), SERVICE(S), TACTIC(S), TECHNIQUES AND/OR IDEA(S) DISCUSSED, DESCRIBED, MENTIONED IN OUR MATERIAL AND/OR ON OUR WEBSITES, VIDEO(S) AND SOCIAL MEDIA ACCOUNTS WILL ACHIEVE ANY RESULTS AT ALL. YOU ARE RESPONSIBLE FOR YOUR OWN ACTIONS.

Federal Trade Commission Required Disclaimer

To better define the term "average" and/or "typical" results, we will attempt to collect results from individuals that have completed courses, trainings, programs, seminars, live presentations or any other platform that can be construed as informational. It is understandable that some individuals that have purchased a course, product(s), service(s), tactic(s), techniques and/or idea(s) discussed or described may have never even used or opened the material, therefore unfortunately would have no results at all.

All of the testimonials, stories, case studies and/or presented results and any other supporting materials related to the potential success by using any of the course, product(s), service(s), tactic(s), techniques and/or idea(s) discussed or described, does not mean anyone current, past or in the future will have any results at all. We do not guarantee anything. There is no guarantee, expressly, implied, inadvertently offered or even suggested for anyone purchasing and/or using our course(s), product(s), service(s), tactic(s), techniques and/or idea(s) discussed or described.

The testimonials, stories, case studies and/or presented examples in any of the Ligon Brothers materials represent what can be achieved, however it should be assumed by the student, client, reader, etc. that the results are based solely on the capability of the student and may not be reproducible by all.

The testimonials, stories, case studies and/or presented results and any other supporting materials related to the potential success are based on many variables and cannot be accurately quantified to meet the advertising standards set forth by the Federal Trade Commission (FTC) for determining the calculation of "average" and/or "typical results. Because of this it is unreasonable that any student should assume that any course, product(s), service(s), tactic(s), techniques and/or idea(s) discussed or described will produce any results at all especially if they choose not to use it properly and/or consistently.